USA TODAY
CULTURAL MOSAIC

The
Hispanic American
Experience

Sandy Donovan

TF
CB

Twenty-First Century Books · Minneapolis

This book takes a broad look at Hispanic Americans. However, like all cultural groups, the Hispanic American community is extremely diverse. Each member of this community relates to his or her background and heritage in different ways, and each has had a different experience of what it means to be Hispanic American.

Twenty-First Century Books
A division of Lerner Publishing Group, Inc.
241 First Avenue North
Minneapolis, MN 55401 U.S.A.

Website address: www.lernerbooks.com

Library of Congress Cataloging-in-Publication Data

Donovan, Sandra, 1967–
     The Hispanic American Experience / by Sandy Donovan.
        p.   cm. — (USA TODAY cultural mosaic)
     Includes bibliographical references and index.
     ISBN 978-0-7613-4085-0 (lib. bdg. : alk. paper)
     1. Hispanic Americans—History. 2. Hispanic Americans—Social life and customs.
   I. Title.
   E184.S75D66 2011
   973'.0468—dc22   2009016370

Manufactured in the United States of America
1 – DP – 7/15/10

USA TODAY

CULTURAL MOSAIC

WITHDRAWN

The number of Hispanic Americans in the United States is growing. Hispanics make up about 15 percent of the U.S. population.

INTRODUCTION:

A PROUD TRADITION

H ispanic Americans have a long and proud tradition in the United States. The Spanish were among the first Europeans to arrive in the Americas. At one point, the Spanish ruled nearly all the countries in Central and South America. And many Spanish people lived in what is now the United States. A large number of modern Hispanic Americans are the descendants of those original Spanish settlers. Most are also the descendants of Native American peoples.

Hispanics make up about 15 percent of the U.S. population. The largest group of Hispanic Americans is Mexican Americans. Some are the descendants of Mexican people who lived in the Southwest when it became part of the United States. Others immigrated many generations ago. Still others left Mexico in recent times to seek new opportunities in the United States.

Hispanic Americans also include Cubans, Dominicans, Puerto Ricans, and people from other Latin American countries. Many fled their home countries to escape war, poverty, or violence. They may be new arrivals, or their families may have lived and prospered in the United States for generations. No matter what their background, Hispanic Americans are a vital part of American society in the twenty-first century. This book will look at who they are, where they've been, and where they're going.

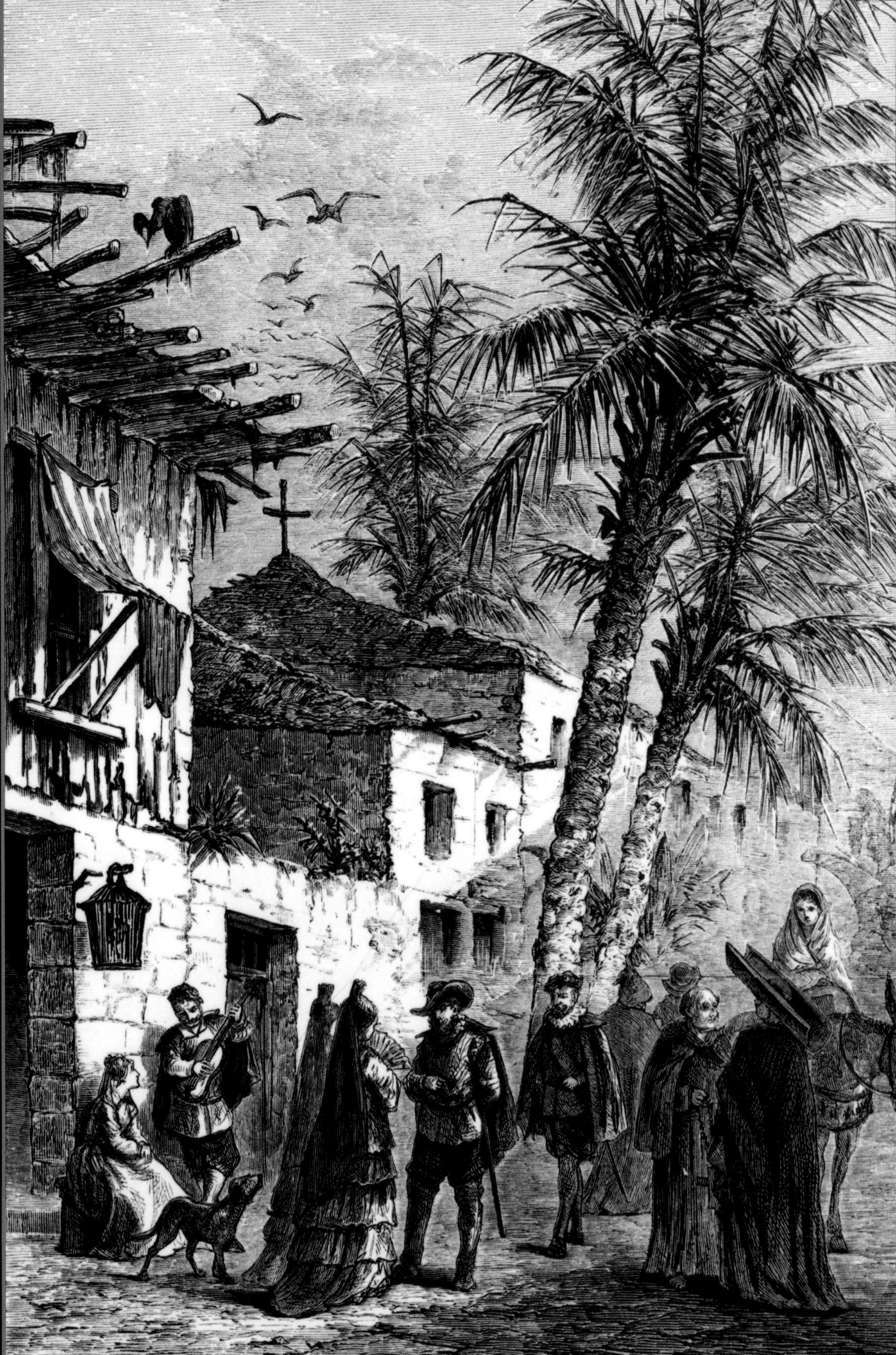

CHAPTER 1:
LANGUAGE AND LITERATURE
EN ESPAÑOL

Hispanic Americans have roots in more than a dozen countries. They have diverse cultural traditions and backgrounds. But they have one thing in common: they either speak Spanish or have ancestors who spoke Spanish.

Spanish was the first European language spoken in the Americas. Spanish explorers reached the Americas in the late 1400s. They traveled throughout the present-day United States for the next several hundred years. They established some of the area's first cities and gave them Spanish names. These included Santa Fe in what is now New Mexico and Saint Augustine in what is now Florida. Many other U.S. states and cities have Spanish names also. Colorado means "red rock," and Los Angeles means "the angels."

OPPOSITE PAGE: This illustration shows Spanish settlers in Saint Augustine, Florida, in the early 1500s. Saint Augustine is the oldest city in the United States in which people have continually lived.

THIS PAGE: This drawing shows Sante Fe, New Mexico, in the mid-1800s.

THE FIRST SPANISH-SPEAKING AMERICANS

English people first arrived in the Americas in 1620. Over the next century, thousands settled in North America. They established colonies where English was the official language. In 1776 the United States declared its independence from Great Britain. English was the official language of the new country. But in other parts of the Americas, Spanish people continued to settle. They came to Central America, South America, and to the part of North America that became Mexico. Some Spanish settlers married Native Americans. The native peoples spoke many different languages. When they traveled or relocated to new areas, they often could not communicate with other native peoples. But many learned Spanish. Soon the Spanish language became a common thread.

By the 1800s, Spanish was the official language of Mexico. At the time, Mexico was more than twice its present size. In the 1840s, the United States acquired a giant piece of land from Mexico as a result of the Mexican-American War (1846–1848). This included the present-day states of California, Utah, and Nevada. It also included parts of New Mexico, Arizona, Colorado, and Wyoming. Along with the new lands came many Spanish speakers. Many rivers, towns, and cities had Spanish names.

In the late 1800s, many Spanish-speaking immigrants began arriving in the United States. They came from Mexico and other Latin American countries. They most often moved to the United States to escape poverty in their home countries. When they arrived, they seldom spoke English. Often they built Spanish-speaking communities. But usually they learned English at their new jobs. Their children learned English in school. Most of the descendants of these early Spanish-speaking immigrants no longer speak Spanish. But their

A Country or a Continent?

Many people are unclear about what Latin America is. Is it a country? Is it a continent? And where is it on a map?

Actually, Latin America is neither a country nor a continent. It isn't just one place that you can point to on a globe. It is a name for a region that includes all the Spanish-speaking lands (plus Brazil) in the Western Hemisphere south of the United States.

The entire continent of South America is part of Latin America. And all the countries in Central America are part of Latin America too. Belize, Costa Rica, El Salvador, Guatemala, and Honduras are among these.

Some Caribbean countries are Latin American. These include Cuba, Haiti, and Martinique. The United States is not part of Latin America. But one U.S. territory is part of Latin America: Puerto Rico.

grandparents and great-grandparents left their mark on everyday language in the United States. Most Americans know that *amigo* means "friend" and *siesta* means "nap."

NEWER ARRIVALS

In the 1900s, more Spanish speakers arrived in the United States. Most continued to come from Mexico. But in the 1950s, many arrived from the small country of Cuba. Cuba is an island in the Caribbean Sea. In 1959 political revolutionary Fidel Castro and his followers overthrew Cuba's dictator. They established a new Communist government. Many Cubans did not agree with Castro's ideas for the country. They decided to leave their country rather than live under

Castro's rule. Since Castro took power, more than one million Cubans have moved to the United States. They established Spanish-speaking communities in South Florida and New York, which continue to thrive.

A few decades later, Spanish speakers began arriving from countries in Central America. In the 1980s and 1990s, violent wars raged in El Salvador, Guatemala, and Nicaragua. To get away from the violence, many people immigrated to the United States. These days, almost two million people from Central America live in the United States. Since most of them arrived relatively recently, they still speak Spanish. Spanish speakers have also immigrated to the United States from Spanish-speaking countries in South America. These include Argentina, Colombia, Ecuador, Venezuela, and others.

USA TODAY Snapshots®

Most foreign-born from Latin America

The nation's foreign-born population increased from 33.5 million in 2003 to 34.2 million in 2004, accounting for 12% of the U.S. total population. Breakdown by region (in millions):

Europe[1] 4.7

Asia 8.7

Other regions 2.6

Latin America 18.3

1 — Russian-born are considered "European" for this analysis

Source: Census Bureau   By Shannon Reilly and Dave Merrill, USA TODAY, 2008

This *USA TODAY* Snapshot shows how many people immigrated to the United States from Latin America in 2004. Even more have immigrated since then. The number of U.S. Spanish speakers continues to grow.

HISTORY OF PREJUDICE

Spanish speakers in the United States have faced prejudice from the beginning. When the United States acquired the Spanish-speaking territories of California and the Southwest, it appointed English speakers to run the new territorial governments. English-speaking

Americans began to move to these areas. Many did not want to learn Spanish. Some would not do business with Spanish speakers. Schools were not allowed to teach in Spanish. Laws were written in English. As a result, many Spanish speakers did not understand the laws.

This discrimination caused many Spanish speakers to stick close together. Some created their own Spanish-speaking communities. Some started their own Spanish-language schools. They published Spanish-language newspapers.

More recent immigrants have moved to Spanish-speaking communities as well. They do this partly because of the discrimination they face as Spanish speakers. But they also like the reminders of home that they find with others who speak Spanish.

Spanish-speaking communities are often called barrios, which means "neighborhood." One of the most famous U.S. barrios is the area around Olvera Street in East Los Angeles. Olvera Street includes Mexican-style buildings that were built in the 1700s by the city's first European settlers. In modern times, the area is a tourist attraction.

A shopper looks over leather goods at a shop on Olvera Street in East Los Angeles, California. The area around Olvera Street features historic Mexican-style buildings and many shops that attract tourists.

It features a huge marketplace in an open-plaza area. Many Hispanic Americans live in other barrios throughout East Los Angeles.

In New York City, many Puerto Ricans and other Hispanic Americans live in Spanish Harlem. In Miami, Florida, Calle Ocho is home to Cuban immigrants. Many other major U.S. cities have large and small barrios that Hispanic Americans call home. Recent immigrants as well as second- and third-generation Americans live in barrios. In these neighborhoods, Hispanic Americans can get a small taste of their home countries' cultures. Perhaps most important, they can speak, listen, and read in their home language of Spanish.

Because of discrimination, many Hispanic American parents did not encourage their children to use Spanish. This was especially true in the early 1900s—a time when people tended to value assimilation (blending into mainstream culture). At that time, many Hispanic American parents feared that speaking Spanish would hurt their children's chances for success in the United States. Consequently, many second- and third-generation Hispanic Americans no longer speak Spanish.

These days, Hispanic American parents are more likely to support their children's use of Spanish. In fact, some may make extra efforts to speak Spanish in their homes so that their children understand the language of their ancestors.

From the Pages of USA TODAY

English rates first in Latino families

When I was growing up, there was a subject around home that made everyone uncomfortable. It was a dark secret that my relatives didn't like to talk about, although it affected many Mexican-American families just like ours. The source of this embarrassment was the fact that my brothers and I didn't speak Spanish. Worse, we didn't care about speaking Spanish.

As it turns out, most families who are descended from Latino [Hispanic] immigrants share our experience. A study published last year in the journal *Population and Development Review* found that, within a few generations of families moving to the USA, Spanish dies out and English becomes the dominant language. Given this reality, it's xenophobic to view the Spanish language as a threat to American society.

Even so, just last weekend Newt Gingrich [a conservative politician] denounced bilingual education by saying, "People (should) learn the common language of the country . . . the language of prosperity, not the language of living in a ghetto."

His comments are as offensive as they are misguided. According to a 2006 survey by the Pew Center [a research organization], 57 percent of Hispanics believe that immigrants have to speak English to be part of American society, while 41 percent did not. Pew also found that an overwhelming 92 percent of Latinos thought it was "very important" for the children of immigrants to be taught English.

When my grandpa arrived from Mexico in 1914, he immediately set about learning the English language so he could find work. While my mother grew up in a bilingual barrio household, she and her sisters preferred English. One generation later, my mom was suggesting that I watch the Spanish-language news on TV, to broaden my vocabulary. Back then, I could not have cared less. It was only as an adult that I came to appreciate the beauty of the Spanish language.

Gingrich should know better than to demean the native tongue of Cervantes, Lorca, and Marquez [famous Hispanic writers]. It isn't constructive to promote English by insulting Spanish. As millions of Latinos already know, speaking Spanish has never taken away from our proud American experience. It has only enriched it.

—*Raul Reyes, from the Opinion page*

PROUD LITERARY TRADITION

Hispanic Americans have a proud literary history in both Spanish and English. Latin American authors wrote many of the world's greatest works of literature. Prize-winning Hispanic authors are studied in schools throughout the United States. They include Gabriel García Márquez of Colombia and Isabel Allende of Chile.

One of the first celebrated Hispanic American authors was the Mexican American playwright Luis Valdez. Valdez wrote several plays about the Mexican American experience. For example, his play *Zoot Suit* (1972) tells the story of race riots in Los Angeles in the 1940s. During the riots, some Mexican Americans wore zoot suits—baggy suits with padded shoulders. The term soon became a derogatory reference to Mexican Americans. *Zoot Suit* became the first play written by a Mexican American to open on Broadway in New York. Valdez later wrote the screenplay for a movie version of *Zoot Suit*. He also wrote

Author Isabel Allende is of Chilean descent. She is best known for her books *The House of the Spirits* (1985) and *City of the Beasts* (2002).

Luis Valdez *(right)* is a Mexican American author who wrote the novel *Zoot Suit*, about race riots in Los Angeles in the 1940s. Some participants in the riots dressed in zoot suits, like the one in this photo from 1943 *(left)*.

the screenplay for *La Bamba* (1987). This hit film is based on the life of 1950s Mexican American rock star Ritchie Valens.

The first popular novel by a Mexican American was *Pocho* (1959), by José Antonio Villarreal. This novel tells the story of a young Mexican American growing up in California. The book is partly based on Villarreal's life. He was the son of Mexican American migrant farmworkers in California. The Spanish word *pocho* means "rotting fruit." The term is used by Mexicans to describe Mexican Americans who speak very little Spanish and know little about their Mexican culture.

Down These Mean Streets (1967), an autobiography by Piri Thomas, describes the prejudice and discrimination faced by the Hispanic author. Thomas grew up in New York City's Spanish Harlem. His family has both Puerto Rican and Cuban roots. In his book, he describes how many Americans mistake him for an African American because of his dark skin. He faces both anti-Hispanic and anti-African American racism.

MODERN LATIN AMERICAN AUTHORS

Beginning in the 1970s, more books by Hispanic American authors became best sellers. The novel *Bless Me, Ultima* (1972), by Rudolfo Anaya, was awarded the Premio Quinto Sol (a publishing company) award for outstanding Chicano literature. This book tells the story of a young boy in New Mexico and the *curandera* (traditional healer) who comes to live with him. The book is considered a classic and was the featured novel in the 2009 United States Academic Decathlon, a scholastic competition for high school students. Participants in the decathlon were asked to read Anaya's novel and prepare to answer questions about it. Anaya went on to have a long writing career, publishing dozens of books. Several of his books—including *Elegy on the Death of César Chávez* (2000), *Roadrunner's Dance* (2000), and *The Santero's Miracle: A Bilingual Story* (2004)—are for children.

Award-winning Chicano author Rudolfo Anaya has written books for adults and children.

Sandra Cisneros's prize-winning novel *The House on Mango Street* (1983) is on the reading list of many U.S. high schools.

USA TODAY CULTURAL MOSAIC

Sandra Cisneros

Born in Chicago, Illinois, in 1954, Mexican American novelist Sandra Cisneros *(right)* began writing in high school. She penned poems and edited her school's literary magazine. Cisneros found writing a welcome escape from her family's poverty. She also loved to read and often lost herself in books.

Cisneros studied English in college. She earned a degree from Chicago's Loyola University in 1976. She also attended graduate school and obtained a master's degree in creative writing from the University of Iowa in 1978.

Cisneros is best known for her acclaimed work *The House on Mango Street*, which won an American Book Award in 1985. She has also written several other books, including *My Wicked, Wicked Ways* (1987), *Loose Woman: Poems* (1994), and *Caramelo* (2002). Many of her works deal with social issues such as feminism and oppression.

Cisneros continues to write and is working on several projects, including a fiction collection and a children's story. She is also working on a book about writing, titled *Writing in My Pajamas*.

The book tells the story of a Mexican American girl growing up in Chicago, Illinois. Other notable books by Mexican American authors are *And the Earth Did Not Part* (1971) by Tomas Rivera, *Hunger of Memory* (1982) by Richard Rodriguez, *Bloodroot* (1982) by Alma Villanueva, *So Far from God* (1993) by Ana Castillo, and *The Whole Sky Full of Stars* (2007) by René Saldaña Jr.

Hispanic American writers with roots throughout Latin America have written books, plays, and poems describing the Hispanic American experience. The Puerto Rican poet and professor Miguel Algarín has won three American Book Awards, including awards for the poetry collections *On Call* (1980) and *Time's Now/Ya Es Tiempo* (1985). He also cofounded the Nuyorican (New York-Puerto Rican) Poets Café in New York City, which hosts readings of Puerto Rican American poetry, short stories, and plays. Cuban American writer Oscar Hijuelos became the first Hispanic to win the prestigious Pulitzer Prize for Fiction for *The Mambo Kings Play Songs of Love* (1990). *The Brief Wondrous Life of Oscar Wao* (2007), a first novel

Dominican author Junot Díaz won the Pulitzer Prize in 2008 for his first novel, *The Brief Wondrous Life of Oscar Wao*.

by Junot Díaz, also won the Pulitzer Prize. Díaz was born in the Dominican Republic and immigrated to New Jersey at the age of six.

Peruvian American author Daniel Alarcón has been honored for his writing. Alarcón was named one of twenty-one Best Young American Novelists under thirty-five in 2007 by the literary publication *Granta*. His book *War by Candlelight* (2005) was a finalist for the 2006 PEN/Hemingway Foundation Award. In 2007 Alarcón published his first novel, *Lost Radio City*.

CHAPTER 2:

IN THE ARTS

H ispanic Americans have a long tradition in music and art. Many of the cultural traditions that Hispanic immigrants brought to the United States have found their way into the modern popular arts scene. Hispanic Americans have faced discrimination in many artistic fields. For example, sometimes Hispanic American actors had to change their names or pretend they weren't Hispanic. In modern times, Hispanic Americans are a central part of all aspects of American cultural life. Their contributions to the arts have expanded and enriched the nation's artistic heritage.

A mariachi band plays at a festival in El Paso, Texas. The original mariachi were street musicians in Mexico. Mariachi bands are popular at events all over the United States.

MUSIC

Walk through a barrio in any U.S. city, and you'll hear the many distinctive sounds of Latin music. In fact, music from Spanish-speaking countries is popular throughout the United States. There's dance music such as salsa and mariachi. There's the funky beat of reggaeton, a hip-hop style imported from

Puerto Rico. There's Latin jazz, Latin pop, and "rock en Español"—
or Spanish rock and roll. And Hispanic American musicians have
contributed to just about every other musical style you can name.

Hispanic Americans have made many contributions to American
pop music. As Hispanics immigrated to the United States, they
brought many musical styles from their home countries. From
Mexico came Tejano music. Puerto Ricans brought the world-
famous salsa sound to the United States and the rest of the world.
Cubans brought their own African-influenced tunes. In most Latin
American countries, music is a big part of the culture. Families play
and sing together, and gatherings and celebrations always include
music. When Hispanic immigrants moved to the United States, they
continued to play music and sing in their home language. It was one
way that the new immigrants could hold on to their home culture.

Rock en Español

Throughout the world, most true rock and roll has English lyrics. Rock musicians in France, Germany, Japan, and other countries often sing in English
even if they don't understand the language. Record companies say this music
sells better than music sung in French, German, or Japanese. But beginning
in the 1990s, many rock bands in Spain, South America, and Central America
began singing in Spanish. They called their style rock en Español. Today, rock
en Español bands draw huge crowds in Spanish-speaking countries and the
United States. U.S. rock en Español bands such as Maria Fatal, Los Olvidados,
and King Chango regularly fill stadiums when they perform.

In the mid-1900s, several Latin music stars became extremely popular in the United States. In the 1950s, Tito Puente was known as the King of Latin Music. He also had the nickname Mambo King. The son of Puerto Rican immigrants, Puente grew up in New York City and became a star playing Latin jazz in New York nightclubs. As his fame grew across the United States, Puente introduced Latin American and Caribbean music to Americans. He went on to win five Grammy awards in his fifty-year music career.

Since the mid-twentieth century, many Hispanic Americans have topped the U.S. pop charts. In 1958 Mexican American Ritchie Valens scored a number-one hit with "La Bamba." The song, which he sang in Spanish, is an old Mexican folk tune. Ten years later, another Mexican American named Carlos Santana began climbing the charts. Santana was born in Mexico and moved to California with his family at the age of thirteen. For more than forty years, Santana has been a huge presence in U.S. pop music. He sings in both Spanish and English. In addition to pop, he has recorded Latin jazz, blues, Afro-Cuban rhythms, and rock.

Los Lobos is a Hispanic American band from California. The

Mexican American musician Carlos Santana has been making hit records for more than forty years. His recent albums have been collaborations with the most popular artists of the day.

band is made up of a group of friends from an East Los Angeles barrio. Throughout the 1970s, they gained a huge following in the barrio. By the 1980s, they were one of the most successful pop acts in the United States. They recorded songs in English and Spanish, including a remake of Ritchie Valens's "La Bamba." Since then they've sold millions of albums around the world.

Many Hispanic pop stars are household names in the United States. Some rose to fame in the 1990s. Selena was one of these. This enormously popular singer specialized in Latin-flavored pop. She performed throughout the country until 1995, when the mentally disturbed president of her fan club fatally shot her. Pop stars Ricky Martin and Gloria Estefan also gained fame in the 1990s. They sing in both Spanish and English. Martin was born in Puerto Rico and moved to New York after becoming a pop sensation in his teens. Estefan was born in Cuba and came with her family to Florida when she was sixteen months old. Both stars are credited with popularizing Latin music in the United States.

From the Pages of USA TODAY

Selena returned me to my Mexican roots

Growing up, my cousin Becka used to tell me that I was a lousy Chicano. I didn't like rice and beans, which in my Mexican-American household we ate with nearly every meal. I couldn't wait to get away from East Los Angeles. And I wouldn't have been caught dead listening to Latin music; I couldn't understand all of the words anyway.

Once I left home, however, I became an unlikely convert to Selena fandom. Flipping around the late-night TV dial, I'd catch sight of the pop singer on the Spanish-language variety shows. With her full, red lips and cascading dark hair, Selena was charismatic, sexy, and still a lot like the chica next door.

Her music reminded me of rhythms I associated with my grandpa's house in El Paso [Texas], melodies I once would've considered hokey. Selena infused these traditional [songs] with an updated, infectious pop sound. It was Tejano music—part Texan, part Mexican—and I was surprised at how much I'd been missing.

Today, a day after the 10th anniversary of her murder, I miss Selena herself.

I still remember the Hispanic outpouring of grief. To her Hispanic fans, Selena was more than the sum of her accomplishments. She was one of us, straddling two cultures and loving both of them.

Selena was a girl from el barrio who remained true to her roots. Despite her wealth, she mowed her own lawn, ate at Pizza Hut, and lived two doors down from her parents in a working-class neighborhood.

I see sad irony in the short life of Selena Quintanilla Perez. Although she introduced Tejano music to a wide audience, her superstardom was a result of her tragic death. Her passing came right on the cusp of the emergence of Hispanics as a powerful, visible minority group.

"Como La Flor," like a flower—the title of one of her biggest hits—Selena bloomed beautifully and briefly. Yet, I'll always be grateful to her for helping me reconnect with my own heritage. She made me a better Chicano, and these days, I'm awfully proud of that.

—Raul Reyes, from the Opinion page

Christina Aguilera is well known for her pop music songs, but she has also done a Spanish album.

Other Hispanic Americans, such as the rapper B-Real of Cypress Hill, mix a Latin sound into hip-hop and rap music. B-Real was born in Los Angeles to a Mexican mother and a Cuban father. His band Cypress Hill became the best-selling Latin rap group in the 1990s and early 2000s. Christina Aguilera is another chart topper with Latin American roots. Her father is from Ecuador. Aguilera became famous in the 1990s for bubblegum pop—fun, upbeat music that appeals to teens and preteens. But later, she began emphasizing her Hispanic roots. In 2000 she released an album in Spanish. Puerto Rican American singer and actress Jennifer Lopez has made a splash in the music world too. Her debut album, *On the 6*, came out in 1999 and quickly became one of the year's top hits. Lopez followed up with several other popular recordings, including *J. Lo* and *Rebirth*.

ON THE SCREEN

Hispanic American actors and actresses have enjoyed huge success in the United States. But in the early years, they often had to hide the fact that they were Hispanic. In the 1930s, a dark-haired Hispanic American named Rita Cansino made several movies. She did not receive much attention. But by the 1940s, she

Movie star Rita Cansino changed her name to Rita Hayworth in the 1940s.

had dyed her hair auburn and changed her last name to the English-sounding Hayworth. Rita Hayworth became one of Hollywood's leading stars. But few of her fans even knew that she was Hispanic. A decade later, another Hispanic American with an English-sounding name—Anthony Quinn—became a Hollywood star. Quinn's name came from his Irish father, but his mother was Mexican.

Over the following decades, many more Hispanic American actors and actresses have become Hollywood stars. Rosie Perez grew up in a

America Ferrera

Honduran American actress America Ferrera *(right)* shot to fame in the television comedy series *Ugly Betty*. Born in Los Angeles, California, in 1984, Ferrera dreamed of acting at an early age. By the time she was in high school, she was trying out for roles in plays all over Los Angeles.

When Ferrera was eighteen, she landed her first role in a movie. The film—called *Gotta Kick It Up!*—played on the Disney Channel. Over the next several years, Ferrera earned many more roles in movies and on television. In 2006 she got her big break with the role of Betty Suarez in *Ugly Betty*, a show that Hispanic American actress Salma Hayek helps produce. In the show, Ferrera plays a girl that everybody thinks is unattractive. In 2007 Ferrera won a Golden Globe Award for Best Performance by an Actress in a Television Series Comedy or Musical. She also earned a 2007 Screen Actors Guild Award for Best Female Actor in a Comedy Series.

USA TODAY
CULTURAL MOSAIC

Puerto Rican family in Brooklyn, New York. At the age of twenty-one, she became a star in the film *Do the Right Thing* (1989). Perez played the main character's Hispanic girlfriend in the movie. She paved the way for other Hispanics to take on Hispanic roles.

Salma Hayek followed in Perez's footsteps. Hayek has played many Hispanic parts throughout the years. Hayek was born in Mexico and began acting on Mexican television shows. She moved to California in the 1990s and became a star in the hit film *Desperado* (1995). Hayek dreamed of making a movie about the Mexican artist Frida Kahlo. She spent many years working toward that goal. In 2002 the movie *Frida* was released. Hayek both produced and starred in it. The film won two Academy Awards (for Best Makeup and Best Music, Original Score) and received six Academy Award nominations—including one for Hayek's role as Frida.

Hispanic American actors Cameron Diaz and Wilmer Valderrama have not played Hispanic roles. However, both have spoken publicly about their pride in their Hispanic heritage. Diaz gets her fair complexion and blue eyes from her German mother. Her

Actress Cameron Diaz is the daughter of a Cuban American father and a German mother.

Hispanic roots come from her Cuban American father. Valderrama, who starred on the television comedy *That '70s Show*, was born in Miami. Both of his parents are from South America. His mother is from Colombia, and his father is from Venezuela. The family lived in Venezuela from the time Wilmer was three until he was thirteen. In 2009 Valderrama partnered with the Congressional Hispanic Caucus Institute to serve as spokesperson for the Ready to Lead college readiness program. The program promotes higher education for Hispanic youth.

Wilmer Valderrama is best known for the role of Fez on *That '70s Show*. He has also starred in movies and is the voice of Manny on the Disney cartoon series *Handy Manny*.

ART AND ARCHITECTURE

Many Hispanic American artists have brought influences from their home countries to their new homes. For instance, Mexico has a rich history of murals—large, colorful works of art painted on walls. In Mexico, murals are seen as a way of connecting all people to important political and social ideas. Diego Rivera (1886–1957) was one of the country's best-known muralists. In the United States, Mexican American artist Judy Baca has carried on the tradition of

USA TODAY
CULTURAL MOSAIC

Artist Judy Baca carries on the Mexican tradition of mural painting. Here she stands in front of *The Great Wall of Los Angeles*, which she helped create in Los Angeles, Callifornia. The mural, one of the longest in the world, depicts California history from the beginning of time to the 1950s.

mural painting. Baca was born in California and studies painting in both the United States and Mexico. In the late 1980s, she led a citywide project in Los Angeles that hired more than one thousand poor youths to paint eighty murals throughout the city. In 1998 she organized a traveling mural dedicated to world peace called *The World Wall: A Vision of the Future without Fear*.

Many Hispanic Americans have made their mark in the art world. The pop-art painter Jean-Michel Basquiat was born in New York City to a Puerto Rican mother and Haitian father. Basquiat became famous for his graffiti art in the late 1970s. By the 1980s, he had gained respect as a serious artist and had shows at many top New York City galleries. Much of his art explores the theme of racism in the United States. Basquiat died in 1988.

Tony Mendoza is a Cuban American photographer. He is most famous for his book *Ernie* (1985), which tells the story in photographs of a cat he met when he moved into a New York City apartment. Mendoza has won three fellowships from the National Endowment for the Arts.

Robert Graham was a famous Mexican American sculptor. He is well known for large monument-style sculptures of the human body. In 1984 he designed the ceremonial gateway for the Olympic Coliseum in Los Angeles. In 1992 he married film star Anjelica Huston, and he later made a cameo appearance in her movie *The Life Aquatic with Steve Zissou* (2004). In 2008 he was inducted into the California Hall of Fame. He died just twelve days later.

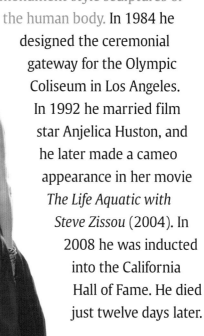

Mexican American sculptor Robert Graham poses with his wife, actress Anjelica Huston, in this 2007 photo.

The Petronas Twin Towers in Kuala Lumpur, Malaysia *(left)*, were designed by Hispanic American architect Cesar Pelli *(right)*.

Hispanic Americans have made many contributions in the world of architecture. In South America, architecture is a highly valued art form. One of the most famous South American architects is Cesar Pelli. Pelli was born in 1926 in San Miguel de Tucumán, Argentina, and immigrated to the United States at the age of forty-six. He has designed famous buildings around the world, including the Petronas Twin Towers in Kuala Lumpur, Malaysia, which were the world's tallest buildings from 1998 to 2004. Pelli also designed the World Financial Center towers in New York City.

Baseball pitcher Pedro Martinez is just one of many Hispanic Americans who are on professional baseball teams.

CHAPTER 3:

PLAY BALL!

Take a look at the names printed on the players' jerseys in any Major League Baseball game. You might see something interesting: lots of Hispanic names, such as Martinez and Rodriguez. There are a lot of Hispanic baseball players in the United States. Hispanics make up just 15 percent of the U.S. population, but Major League Baseball teams are about 30 percent Hispanic. Some Hispanic players grew up in the United States. Others were discovered in their home countries by scouts for Major League Baseball. Baseball scouts often travel to countries in Latin America. They go to local baseball games to look for top-notch players.

USA TODAY Olympic Snapshots®

Cuban domination

Cuba is the only team to medal in all four Olympic baseball competitions, including three golds, and has averaged nearly nine runs a game.
Most runs scored:

Cuba 313
Japan 261
USA 203
Italy 110
Taiwan 91

Source: *The Complete Book of the Olympics*

By Kevin Greer and Sam Ward, USA TODAY, 2008

Latin America is home to many talented baseball players. This *USA TODAY* Snapshot shows Cuba's success in Olympic baseball competitions.

A BASEBALL TRADITION

Baseball has long been a favorite sport in Latin America—and Latin American players have a long history in U.S. baseball. In 1871 the Cuban player Esteban Bellán became the first Hispanic to play in the U.S. major leagues.

For more than fifty years after that, few Hispanics made it to major-league ball clubs. In the first half of the twentieth century, Major League Baseball was almost exclusively played by white men. But in 1947, Jackie Robinson broke baseball's color barrier. He became the first African American to play in the major leagues. After that, baseball teams started to include more African American and Hispanic players.

Roberto Clemente was one of the earliest and most respected Hispanic players. Clemente played for the Pittsburgh Pirates from 1955 until his tragic death in a plane crash in 1972. In 1973 he became the first Hispanic to be voted into baseball's Hall of Fame.

Gradually, more and more Hispanics began playing baseball. Some of the earliest Hispanics to join Clemente in the Hall of Fame were Juan Mariachal of the Dominican Republic, Luis Aparicio of Venezuela, Rod Carew of Panama, Orlando Cepeda of Puerto Rico, and Tony Perez of Cuba. Since then dozens of Hispanics have become baseball greats. In Miami, Florida, there's a street named after baseball star Jose Canseco. Canseco is a Cuban American player. He played for the Oakland Athletics from 1985 to 1992 and again in 1997. He also played for the Texas Rangers, the Boston Red Sox, the Toronto Blue Jays, the Tampa Bay Devil Rays, and the New York Yankees before making his last major-league appearance in 2001 with the Chicago White Sox. Other Latin American baseball notables include Pedro Martinez, Manny Ramirez, and David Ortiz.

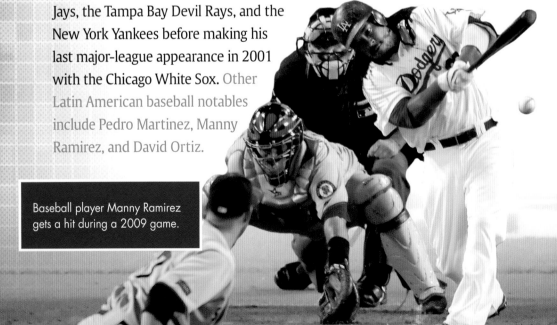

Baseball player Manny Ramirez gets a hit during a 2009 game.

Roberto Clemente

Hall of Fame baseball player Roberto Clemente *(left)* was born in Puerto Rico in 1934. He grew up with six older brothers and sisters and a love of baseball. Clemente played in the Puerto Rican National Baseball League until 1954, when a U.S. baseball scout offered him a chance to play major-league ball. Clemente began playing for the Pittsburgh Pirates in 1955.

In 1966 Clemente won the National League's Most Valuable Player Award. He also won twelve Gold Glove Awards and was chosen to be in the All-Star Game twelve times. Throughout Clemente's baseball career, he remained close to his family in Puerto Rico. He was also very involved in charity work. He helped poor people in Puerto Rico and other Latin American countries.

In December 1972, an earthquake destroyed much of the capital city of Nicaragua. Clemente arranged for food and medicine to be flown to the disaster site. But he soon learned that the first three deliveries were stolen by corrupt government workers. Clemente was heartbroken that the supplies did not reach the victims. He decided that he would fly along with the next delivery to ensure that the supplies would get to those who needed them. Clemente chartered an airplane to fly from Puerto Rico to Nicaragua on New Year's Eve. But the plane crashed just after takeoff. Everyone on board died.

Three months after Clemente died, the Baseball Writers Association of America elected him to the Baseball Hall of Fame. Typically, a player has to be dead or retired for at least five years before he can be elected—but the Baseball Writers Association made an exception to the rules especially for Clemente. In modern times, Major League Baseball awards the Roberto Clemente Award every year to the player who best follows Clemente's example of charity work.

MOVING TO MANAGEMENT

After years of making their mark as Major League Baseball players, Hispanic Americans have recently broken into management. For a long time, almost all major-league managers were white. In 2002 Omar Minaya became the first Hispanic general manager of a Major League Baseball team. He was the Montreal Expos' manager from 2002 until 2004, when he was named general manager for the New York Mets.

In 2002 Omar Minaya became the first Hispanic American general manager in Major League Baseball.

Ozzie Guillen from Venezuela followed in Minaya's footsteps. Guillen was an all-star player for the Chicago White Sox for more than a dozen years in the 1980s and 1990s. After the 2003 season, he became the team's manager.

SOCCER

As popular as baseball is among Hispanic Americans, soccer may have an even bigger following. Soccer—called *futbol* in Spanish-speaking countries—is the national sport in most of Latin America. When Hispanics move to the United States, they often bring along their devotion to soccer. This includes a love of both playing and watching the sport. It's not unusual for extended families and friends to gather to watch an international soccer match on television. In fact, in many Hispanic American communities, World Cup soccer matches are considered major events. If a Latin American country is in the finals, it's like a national holiday for many.

Fans of the Brazilian soccer team watch a World Cup soccer game in Maryland. Fans of soccer teams will often gather to watch their team play on television.

Soccer has grown more and more popular in the United States since the 1970s. It has become the nation's most popular sport for school-age kids to play. Many people say the popularity is due to Hispanic American influence. With more Hispanics living in the United States, more U.S. television stations are broadcasting soccer games. The increased visibility of soccer has attracted a larger number of fans and players to the sport.

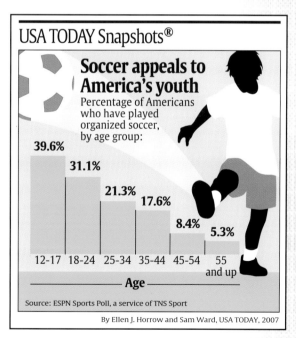

USA TODAY Snapshots®

Soccer appeals to America's youth

Percentage of Americans who have played organized soccer, by age group:

Age	Percentage
12-17	39.6%
18-24	31.1%
25-34	21.3%
35-44	17.6%
45-54	8.4%
55 and up	5.3%

Source: ESPN Sports Poll, a service of TNS Sport

By Ellen J. Horrow and Sam Ward, USA TODAY, 2007

Stephanie Cox

While many Hispanic American soccer stars opt to leave the United States to play for teams in Latin America—where soccer tends to have a bigger following—Mexican American soccer great Stephanie Cox has chosen to pursue her soccer passion closer to home. Cox, born Stephanie Lopez in Los Gatos, California, in 1986, plays for the United States women's national soccer team. She is the first woman of Hispanic descent ever to play for this team.

Cox got her start playing soccer in high school. She helped her team at California's Elk Grove High to two league championships. After high school, Cox attended college at the University of Portland in Oregon. She earned her first call-up to the women's national team in 2005, while still in college. Cox pursued her college education while playing for the women's national team. She graduated in 2007 with a psychology degree and a 3.7 grade point average. That same year, she married her fiancé, Brian Cox—a former baseball player for the University of Portland.

In 2008 Cox and her women's national teammates went to Beijing, China, to play in the Olympic Games. The team beat Brazil 1–0 and took home a gold medal.

BEYOND BASEBALL AND SOCCER

Baseball and soccer aren't the only sports with large numbers of Hispanic American fans. Boxing, golf, and swimming are quite popular as well. In Mexico, boxing is often considered the national sport. Mexican American Oscar de la Hoya won a gold medal in boxing at the 1992 Olympics. He overcame many hardships to achieve this honor.

www.usatoday.com

USA TODAY

Sports
SECTION C

June 13, 2008

From the Pages of USA TODAY

de la Hoya finds balance in life

It took Oscar de la Hoya years to look his opponents in the eye. Now—after co-writing his autobiography, *American Son*—he can face the man in the mirror, too.

"I'm honest and open in this book," says de la Hoya, a six-division world champion. "It was very important for me to make sure that the message is a real message. What I've been through, the times I've been knocked down, it was a tough road. It still is."

TV cameras loved de la Hoya, who became more rock star than athlete. [But] boxing purists often yearned to see him lose. That included fellow Mexican-Americans who [thought] the kid from east Los Angeles, with a perfect smile, manicured look, and perfect English, [must be] a product of privilege.

[In reality, de la Hoya] grew up in a small apartment where roaches were so plentiful that he regarded them as pets. He was derided at school for being poor and wearing the same jeans, sometimes his mother's. The family never ate together and rarely communicated. He never traded "I love yous" with either parent, [a fact] that nags the 35-year-old to this day.

Despite his upbringing, de la Hoya was [still] considered pampered. Sure, he had an anvil of a left hook, but he wasn't cut from the same cloth of Mexican legends such as Salvador Sanchez, Carlos Zarate, Ruben Olivares, or the greatest of all, Julio Cesar Chavez. He's been booed in his hometown. He required police protection because spectators hurled fruit at him in a holiday parade.

The Golden Boy [as de la Hoya has been nicknamed] was making $1 million for a fight just two years into his career. Still, by 1999 he was in financial straits, saddled by multiple lawsuits.

With the help of Swiss banking executive Richard Schaefer, de la Hoya cleaned up his life, and braved it on his own to build an empire through Golden Boy Promotions [de la Hoya's marketing company for athletes]. He also has equity ownership [which means he will share in profits if there are some] of Equal, a sugar substitute.

Indeed, life has never been sweeter. When he locked gazes with longtime nemesis Fernando Vargas in 2002, de la Hoya discarded the last training wheel. He didn't have to look up for help when he knocked out Vargas, the last in a long line of bitter detractors. "People see me as a role model, as hope," says de la Hoya. "Growing up in east L.A., working hard, searching for that American dream, if I can do it anybody can do it."

—*J. Michael Falgoust*

He grew up in poverty and had little support from his parents. More recently, Hispanics have been winning golf and swimming titles. In 2007 swimmer Dara Torres set the U.S. record in the women's 50-meter freestyle. And golfers Angel Cabrera of Argentina and Lorena Ochoa of Mexico won the U.S. Open and the British Open, respectively. The success of these Hispanic stars keeps Hispanic Americans tuned in to sports.

FOOTBALL AND MORE

Some of the most typically American sports—think football and basketball—are also gaining Latin American fans. In October 2005, the National Football League (NFL) played its first regular-season game outside the United States. The game took place in Mexico City, the capital of Mexico.

More than 103,000 fans attended. More and more Hispanic Americans are playing football too. Twenty-five Hispanic American players completed the NFL's

Swimmer Dara Torres set records at the 2008 Summer Olympics in China. At the age of forty-one, Torres was competing in her fifth Olympics. She won three silver medals at the games.

San Antonio Spurs basketball player Manu Ginobili takes the ball to the basket in a game against the Detroit Pistons.

2007–2008 season. They included Kansas City Chiefs tight end Tony Gonzalez, Dallas Cowboys quarterback Tony Romo, Oakland Raiders quarterback Jeff Garcia, and Indianapolis Colts wide receiver Anthony Gonzalez. In the National Basketball Association (NBA), fourteen Hispanic athletes played in 2007–2008. The San Antonio Spurs' Manu Ginobili was among these. This Argentinean player won the Sixth Man Award that season—a prize that sportswriters award to the year's most valuable substitute player.

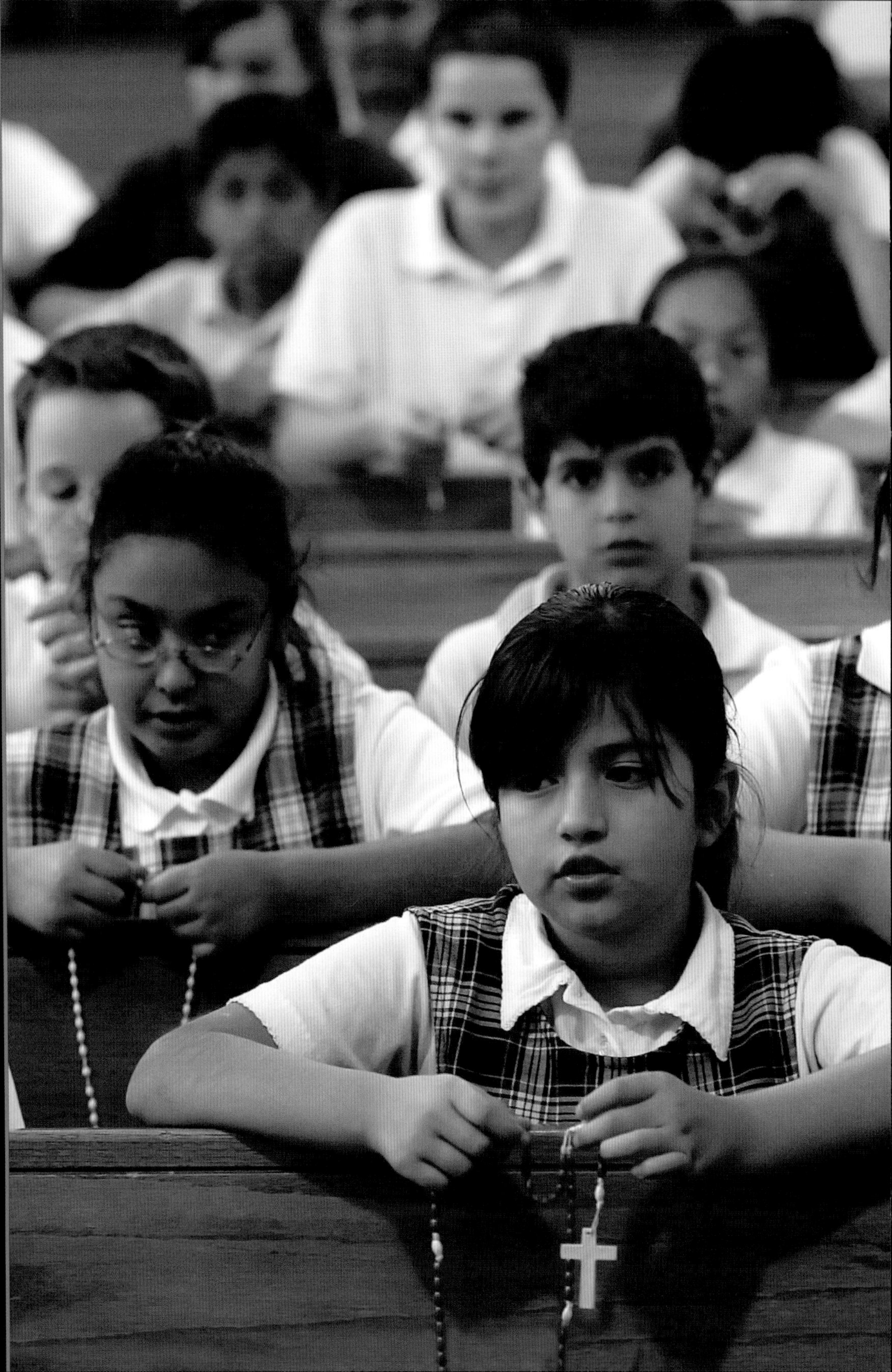

CHAPTER 4:

RELIGIOUS FOCUS

Religion is an important part of life for many Hispanic Americans. Most—but not all—practice Roman Catholicism, a form of Christianity. That's because Spain was a Roman Catholic country when it was building its empire around the world in the 1500s. The Spanish conquerors brought their religion to the countries they settled. They spread their faith among the native peoples in those countries. The result is that, these days, a large number of Latin Americans are Roman Catholic. Latin American immigrants to the United States often bring their faith with them— and they pass their faith on to their children and grandchildren.

HISPANIC AMERICAN CHURCHES

The large number of Roman Catholic churches in many U.S. barrios are a testament to the importance of faith among Hispanic Americans. Los Angeles's Olvera Street, New York City's Spanish Harlem, and Miami's Calle Ocho all have many Roman Catholic churches.

OPPOSITE PAGE: Catholic school students pray at a church in Kansas. The church is made up of 60 percent Hispanic Americans.

THIS PAGE: A Catholic priest in Massachusetts blesses a young Hispanic girl, while her mother looks on.

Enduring Traditions

Before the Spanish spread Roman Catholicism throughout Latin America, people in Latin American had their own religious faiths and customs. Those customs did not disappear once Latin Americans adopted Roman Catholicism. Instead, Latin Americans often combined their customs with Roman Catholic religious practices.

In Guatemala, for example, native peoples mixed their religious rituals with Christian traditions, such as the celebration of Christmas. One result is an annual Christmas mask dance. Worshippers wear colorful masks and costumes to celebrate the Christian holiday.

In Mexico, people in earlier centuries prayed to both the Christian God and their native gods. And to this day, Mexican Roman Catholics revere a holy figure called Our Lady of Guadalupe. Many historians believe she is a mix between the Roman Catholic Virgin Mary (the mother of Jesus Christ) and the native Mexican god Coatlicue. These days, Our Lady of Guadalupe is a common figure in many Roman Catholic churches in Mexican American communities. Many Mexican Americans also have statues of Our Lady of Guadalupe in their homes.

Statues of Our Lady of Guadalupe are a common sight in many Mexican American churches.

USA TODAY
CULTURAL MOSAIC

For many Hispanic Americans, churches are the center of social life. This is especially true for Hispanics who speak little or no English. Often their church is a connection to their home country. It's also a place to speak with others who understand their native language.

Many parishioners, or church members, attend worship services daily. Those who don't go every day usually go on Sundays. Churches get especially crowded on the most important Roman Catholic holidays: Easter and Christmas. During the rest of the year, churches host community and social events. Lunches, dinners, and other nonreligious gatherings are common. And family celebrations such as weddings and funerals are held at local churches.

Roman Catholicism

Roman Catholicism is one of the world's largest religions. More than one-sixth of the world's population belongs to this faith. Roman Catholics, like all Christians, believe in one God, who is represented by three beings: the Father, the Son (Jesus), and the Holy Spirit. Many Roman Catholics attend church regularly. They call their church service a Mass.

The Roman Catholic Church traces its roots back to the life of Jesus. Its official headquarters is the Vatican, near Rome, Italy. Most European countries have had large Roman Catholic populations for centuries. Spain, France, and other Roman Catholic countries colonized (settled) many parts of the world during the sixteenth to eighteenth centuries. During this time, they spread the Roman Catholic religion to North America, South America, and Central America.

A cross and a U.S. flag sit on a stage in an unfinished part of Templo Calvario Church in Santa Ana, California. The church constructed a new area to hold services and made other improvements to house its ever-growing population.

Templo Calvario in Santa Ana, California, is one of the largest Hispanic churches in the United States. The population of Santa Ana is more than 75 percent Hispanic. On many weekdays, more than six thousand people worship at the church. The city of Santa Ana is also one of the poorest cities in the nation. In response, Templo Calvario has set up a food shelf, also known as a food pantry. The food shelf serves hundreds of people each week. Local Hispanic Americans who can afford to donate food and money keep the food shelf running. Each year, Templo Calvario gives away more than $10 million in food and other help to poor residents of Santa Ana.

USA TODAY
CULTURAL MOSAIC

Profile of a Hispanic American Catholic Church

Immaculate Heart of Mary is the oldest Hispanic American Roman Catholic church in Phoenix, Arizona. Mexican immigrants built the church in 1928, after facing severe discrimination at the local Roman Catholic church. At that church, Hispanic worshippers were forced to sit in the basement during services.

In modern times, Immaculate Heart of Mary is a thriving church community. Some of its members are the relatives of the original founders. Many are second- or third-generation Americans. But many are also recent immigrants.

Each Sunday about five thousand parishioners attend one of the church's seven Spanish-language masses. After the services, many worshippers stay for the weekly bazaar, or market. Mexican food and small religious items are for sale in a line of stalls. Church members also spend the hours after church eating and visiting with one another.

Father Ruben Rios, a native of Argentina, speaks to the congregation during Mass at Immaculate Heart of Mary Church in Phoenix, Arizona.

CHANGING TRADITIONS

As more and more Hispanic Americans become assimilated into U.S. culture, some have become less connected to the Roman Catholic Church. They may not look to church to fulfill spiritual or social needs. Or they may look to religions other than Roman Catholicism to help guide them in their faith.

According to a study published in *USA Today*, a smaller percentage of Hispanic Americans called themselves Roman Catholic in 2001 than in 1990. Some—nearly 14 percent—said they have no religion. That's about the same percentage as the U.S. population as a whole. The same study showed that more Hispanic Americans are joining churches other than the Roman Catholic Church. Most are joining Protestant churches. In particular, Hispanic membership is growing in U.S. Baptist and evangelical churches. In Texas alone, there are more than eleven hundred Hispanic Baptist churches serving more than 125,000 Hispanic Americans.

Like Hispanic Roman Catholic churches, many Hispanic Baptist churches seek to help poor Hispanic Americans. Many of the Hispanic Baptist churches in Texas have a program that helps young adults prepare for and take the General Educational Development (GED) test. This test certifies that the test taker has academic skills equal to those of a high school graduate. Hispanic Americans and others who did not graduate from high school but pass this test can more easily qualify for jobs and go on to college.

USA TODAY.
CULTURAL MOSAIC

www.usatoday.com

USA TODAY

Life
SECTION D

January 4, 2003

From the Pages of USA TODAY

More Hispanic Catholics losing their religion

The Catholic Church appears to be losing its grip on Hispanics in the USA. And while some are joining other churches, the fastest-growing religion among Hispanics is no religion at all.

Latin America has been overwhelmingly Catholic since colonial times, and Hispanics in the USA have traditionally held to that religion, says Anthony Stevens-Arroyo, a professor at Brooklyn College and co-founder and director of the Program for the Analysis of Religion Among Latinos. But in the USA, that is changing, according to a study out today based on findings from the *American Religious Identification Survey 2001* (ARIS). The research was commissioned by Stevens-Arroyo's program. The ARIS authors looked at how religious identification has changed in the Hispanic community from 1990 to 2001.

The U.S. Hispanic adult population nearly doubled from 1990 to 2000, to 23 million from 14.6 million. And while the majority still call themselves Catholic, the percentage is dropping. It's down from 66 percent in 1990 to 57 percent in 2001. At the same time, the percentage who said they had no religion more than doubled over the same period—to 13 percent from 6 percent.

But just because more Hispanics are turning away from organized religion doesn't mean they are shunning faith: 53 percent of those who said they have no religion also said they "strongly believe" in God. Only 4 percent professed a strong disbelief in God.

Felipe Chavez, who came to the USA from Mexico at age 10, [was raised as a] Catholic. But when Chavez went to college, his beliefs began shifting. He still attends church for traditional ceremonies such as weddings and funerals, but he no longer considers himself Catholic.

"I'm still spiritual," says Chavez, 31. "I definitely believe there is a higher power. It's the church I distance myself from. I don't go by the book."

But many Hispanics—especially those living in areas without traditional Hispanic communities—responded "no religion" because they don't have a church they can attend, says Stevens-Arroyo. [Growing] Hispanic communities are hungry for churches that can provide community as well as religious guidance. "Our people are very religious. It's just that the Catholic Church hasn't caught up with the people," he says.

—*Janet Kornblum*

These women and girls take part in a celebration for Museo Alameda in San Antonio, Texas. Visitors to the museum can learn about the contributions Hispanics have made to the cultural heritage of the United States.

CHAPTER 5

COLORFUL CELEBRATIONS

B right colors, lively music, and tasty food are key ingredients in Hispanic American celebrations. Many of these celebrations are Roman Catholic holidays such as Christmas and Easter. Others have to do with events in the history of Latin American countries. And one special celebration—National Hispanic Heritage Month—is a four-week commemoration of all the contributions and experiences that Hispanics have brought to the United States.

CELEBRATING RELIGION

Many Hispanics in the United States celebrate Roman Catholic holidays. This is partly because so many Hispanics are Roman Catholic. But it is also because the holidays are a big part of Hispanic tradition. Indeed, many Hispanic Americans who don't consider themselves Roman Catholic still celebrate Roman Catholic holidays.

Christmas is one of the biggest Roman Catholic holidays of the year. Like many U.S. citizens, Hispanic Americans have large celebrations at Christmastime. In fact, many Hispanics begin celebrating almost a month before December 25, the day celebrated as the birth of Jesus. Four Sundays before December 25, Advent begins. The word *advent* comes from the Latin word *aduentus*, which means "coming" or "arrival." During the season of Advent, Christians around the world celebrate the time leading up to the birth of Jesus. In almost all Christian cultures, Advent

celebrations include going to church as well as enjoying festivities with family, food, and music. Gift giving is also part of most Advent celebrations.

In the United States, many Hispanics celebrate Christmas

Advent Wreaths

Many Hispanic American families celebrate the season of Advent with an Advent wreath *(right)*. An Advent wreath looks a lot like a Christmas wreath. It's a circle of pine branches. But instead of hanging it on a door or above a mantle, Hispanic American families lay it flat on a table. They arrange four candles around the wreath. They place one candle in the middle.

The candles are specific colors, and each of them stands for something. Three of the candles around the wreath are purple. They stand for opening one's heart to God. One of the candles around the wreath is rose colored. It stands for joy. The candle in the middle is white. It's called the Christ Candle. The Christ Candle stands for purity. Families don't light it until Christmas Day.

Hispanic Americans take part in the Three Kings Day parade and celebration in Hartford, Connecticut, in 2009. Three local businessmen play the part of the three kings on camels.

with the traditions of their home countries. For instance, in most Latin American countries, gifts are not exchanged on Christmas Day. And Santa Claus does not bring them. Children still receive gifts. But they open them on January 6. This day is called Three Kings Day. According to Christian belief, it represents the day that three kings arrived with gifts for the baby Jesus. Many Hispanic American families give their children gifts on Three Kings Day instead of on Christmas. Observing Three Kings Day helps Hispanic Americans maintain ties to their culture.

www.usatoday.com

Money
SECTION B

January 2, 2008

From the Pages of USA TODAY

Retailers embrace Hispanic tradition of Three Kings Day

If you think the holiday shopping season is over, you're wrong. A growing number of retailers are promoting the Hispanic tradition of celebrating Three Kings Day every Jan. 6 as a way to extend the buying season past Christmas and connect with Hispanic customers.

El Dia de los Reyes [Three Kings Day] celebrates the day in Christian tradition when the three wise men visited the baby Jesus. Known as the Epiphany, the day is as important as Christmas in Mexico, Puerto Rico and many Latin American countries. Children put their shoes out the night before or leave grass for the wise men's camels. They wake the next day to unwrap presents. For retailers, that means two more weeks of shopping.

"It used to be that after Christmas, everything was pretty much dead," says Ignacio Hernandez, CEO of MexGrocer. com, which began offering the traditional Rosca de Reyes (King's cake) five years ago. "Now it's still busy."

For the first time, actors dressed as the three wise men began wandering through Florida Mall in Orlando on Sunday and posing with children for photos on a repurposed Santa display. "Now we have three thrones," laughs general

Many other Hispanics living in the United States celebrate Christmas in the style of their new country. They wait for Santa Claus to bring gifts on Christmas Eve. Some families celebrate the traditions of both their home countries and their new country. They may prepare meals in the style of their family's home country—but they also hang up stockings for Santa Claus to fill.

In Latin America, Easter is a bigger holiday than Christmas. But

manager Brian Peters.

Wal-Mart, which began promoting the tradition in a big way last year, is expanding [its Three Kings Day marketing campaign]. This year, the three kings are visiting Wal-Marts in the Southwest, and more than 300 Wal-Marts have displays and products geared to the celebration. And Kmart is sponsoring the Three Kings parade in Miami on Jan. 13 and an appearance by [Hispanic American singer] Jose Feliciano at its Bronx, New York, store Thursday.

"It makes all the business sense in the world if you can extend the selling season," says Alex Lopez Negrete, CEO of Lopez Negrete Communications, the nation's second-largest Hispanic marketing company. The firm worked with Wal-Mart on its Three Kings campaign. "It tells your customers that you know their traditions," Lopez Negrete says. "It makes you relevant to them."

Catching the growing Hispanic market is a goal for many businesses. At 44.3 million people, Hispanics are the largest minority in the USA, according to the [U.S.] Census [Bureau]. They will control an estimated $1.2 trillion in spending power by 2011, a quadruple increase since 1990, according to Mediamark Research.

Promoting Three Kings Day helps retailers compete, says Juan Pablo Quevedo, research director for Images USA, a multicultural marketing firm in Atlanta whose clients include Sears and Kmart. Until recently, the tradition had been dying out as newly arrived Hispanics became assimilated, he says.

But other retailers will follow Wal-Mart's lead, he says. "With Wal-Mart coming into the scenario, things are going to change."

Not all are so sure. Three Kings Day will remain a regional marketing event, says Esther Novak, CEO of VanguardComm, a multicultural marketing firm in New Brunswick, N.J. "It hasn't hit the center of the marketing radar screen, and I'm not sure it will."

—Mindy Fetterman

in the United States, Christmas is a bigger holiday. For traditional Hispanic Americans, Easter remains the most important holiday. According to Christian belief, it is the celebration of the day Jesus rose from death. Many Hispanics celebrate the entire Holy Week, which is the week before Easter. During this week, Catholics often go to church on Monday, Thursday, and especially on Good Friday. For Christians, this day—which falls two days before

Catholic parishioners in San Diego, California, pray during Easter services at Our Lady of Guadalupe Church.

Easter Sunday—marks the day Jesus died. On Easter Sunday, there is another Mass and other church and family events.

CELEBRATING HOME COUNTRIES

Almost all Hispanic Americans have a special celebration of their own home country each year. Cinco de Mayo is one of the largest celebrations of this type. Cinco de Mayo celebrates Mexico and Mexican culture. It falls on May 5. (Cinco de Mayo means "the fifth of May" in Spanish.) May 5 was the day that Mexicans fought off French invaders in 1862. The French had occupied part of Mexico since late 1861, and they were much better armed than the local Mexican troops. This made the May 5 victory all the more important to the Mexican people.

Mexican Americans mark Cinco de Mayo with festivals and celebrations. Festivities include parades, traditional Mexican dancing, colorful displays of Mexican arts and crafts, special music, and plenty of food.

Puerto Rican Constitution Day is a day for Puerto Rican Americans to celebrate their homeland. Puerto Rican Constitution Day takes place each year on July 25. On this day in 1952, Puerto Rico adopted its first constitution. In Puerto Rico, all businesses and schools are closed on Constitution Day. But in the United States, Puerto Ricans who live near or in New York City are more likely to celebrate on the second Sunday in June, when the Puerto Rican Day Parade fills up Fifth Avenue between 44th and 86th streets. This annual festival of food, music, and dancing is the largest Puerto Rican celebration in the world.

Cuban Americans celebrate Cuba on May 20. May 20 is Cuba's Independence Day, the day on which Cubans won their freedom from Spain in 1898. Cuban Americans might mark their home country's independence with concerts, street festivals, and family get-togethers.

A woman waves a Puerto Rican flag while watching the Puerto Rican Day Parade in New York City. The parade celebrates the day Puerto Rico adopted its first constitution.

NATIONAL HISPANIC HERITAGE MONTH

While celebrations of their home countries are important to Hispanic Americans, they also enjoy celebrating Hispanic American culture as a whole. National Hispanic Heritage Month is a time set aside to do just that. During National Hispanic Heritage Month, schools, libraries, and other organizations recognize the contributions of Hispanics to the United States. Some communities have special events. Many libraries feature special displays of Hispanic books and authors. Schools often put on performances of Latin American dance and music.

National Hispanic Heritage Month began as a weeklong celebration in 1968. The middle of September was selected because many Latin American countries celebrate their independence then. September 15 marks the independence of Costa Rica, El Salvador, Guatemala, Honduras, and Nicaragua. Mexico's independence day is September 16, and Chile celebrates independence on September 18. In 1988 the U.S. Congress extended the weeklong celebration to an entire month. Each year, Americans celebrate National Hispanic Heritage Month from September 15 to October 15.

A banner at a National Football League game in Cincinnati, Ohio, promotes Hispanic Heritage Month.

The Quinceañera

For many Hispanic Americans, a girl's fifteenth birthday is a special time. That's because the age of fifteen—*quince* in Spanish—is considered the beginning of adulthood for girls. *Quinceañera* (fifteenth birthday) celebrations are often huge events. Girls and their families plan for this day for months in advance. It's not unusual to hear a twelve- or thirteen-year-old girl talking about her quinceañera plans.

The birthday girl almost always wears an elaborate dress with white lace ruffles. Food, music, and festive clothing are a part of the celebration. Upper- and middle-income families often rent a ballroom and hire a caterer to prepare fancy foods and drinks. In less well-off families, quinceañera celebrations may be less elaborate—but the effect is the same. Special clothes, delicious food, and plenty of music are always a part of the day.

This fifteen-year-old girl waits outside a dance hall in Santa Ana, California. She is dressed up for her quinceañera, a coming-of-age party traditionally held by Hispanic American families when their daughters turn fifteen.

Black beans, rice, and fried ham is a popular dish in Cuba. Rice is a common ingredient in many Latin American dishes.

CHAPTER 6:

FOODS OF MANY FLAVORS

Cooking and food are a big part of any culture, and people who move to a new country usually bring their food traditions with them. For many years, Hispanics have introduced food from all over Latin America to the United States.

Latin American food is diverse. Cubans don't cook or eat in the same style as Colombians. Mexicans don't share many recipes with Peruvians. But there are some similarities. Most Latin American cooking has some Spanish influences. It's also often influenced by African and Native American cooking styles.

There's a difference between traditional Latin American food and the food eaten by Hispanic Americans in modern times. Often Hispanics can't find the ingredients they need to make their favorite recipes in the United States. So they change the recipes slightly. Over time they begin to mix other cooking styles into their own traditions. The results are sometimes a whole new style of food.

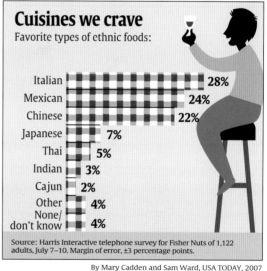

USA TODAY Snapshots®

Cuisines we crave
Favorite types of ethnic foods:

Italian	28%
Mexican	24%
Chinese	22%
Japanese	7%
Thai	5%
Indian	3%
Cajun	2%
Other	4%
None/ don't know	4%

Source: Harris Interactive telephone survey for Fisher Nuts of 1,122 adults, July 7–10. Margin of error, ±3 percentage points.

By Mary Cadden and Sam Ward, USA TODAY, 2007

Mexican food is very popular in the United States. This *USA TODAY* Snapshot shows it's second only to Italian cuisine.

FROM TURKEY MOLE TO CHILI WITH BEANS

It's not hard to find Mexican food anywhere in the United States. Tacos, enchiladas, and burritos are all popular. You can find them in fancy restaurants as well as fast-food joints. But are these foods really Mexican? They are and they aren't. They do include some of the most common ingredients of true Mexican food: rice, beans, tomatoes, and tortillas. But most Mexicans don't eat tacos and burritos for a meal. These foods came from the Native Americans who lived in northern Mexico and the southwestern part of the United States. So these were some of the more common foods in Texas and New Mexico when those areas first became U.S. states.

In most of Mexico, barbecued meat is a popular dinner. In fact, the English word *barbecue* comes from the Spanish word *barbacoa*. In a traditional Mexican barbacoa, a whole goat or lamb cooks for hours over hot coals. Mexicans also make rich sauces to go over meat. Turkey mole is one of the most popular dishes in Mexico. Turkey mole is turkey meat served in a sauce of chili peppers, garlic, onions, bananas, and unsweetened chocolate.

This plate of turkey mole is served with rice and a red tortilla, made from red corn.

USA TODAY. CULTURAL MOSAIC

Salsa

Salsa (Spanish for "sauce") is one of the most popular Mexican American food staples. In fact, Americans buy more salsa than ketchup. Try this easy recipe to make your own salsa. But if you use hot peppers, make sure not to touch your nose or eyes after handling them! You might want to wear rubber gloves when touching the peppers to be extra safe.

INGREDIENTS

6 medium-sized tomatoes, finely chopped
½ small onion, finely chopped
2 tablespoons chopped fresh cilantro
juice of ½ lime
1 teaspoon salt
hot peppers (such as jalapeño, poblano, or Anaheim) to taste, very finely chopped and with seeds removed

PREPARATION

In a large bowl, mix all ingredients together. Cover and refrigerate for at least 1 hour.
Makes about 2 cups

Spicy favorites

How 1,000 people responded when asked, "What's your favorite spicy food?"

Food	Responses
Buffalo wings	278
Salsa	232
Jalapeño peppers	151
Pepper Jack cheese	91
Curry	71
Firehouse chili	64
Other	113

Source: Insight Express survey of 1,000 adults in December 2005

By Adrienne Lewis, USA TODAY, 2006

May 10, 1993

From the Pages of USA TODAY

From desperation, an empire: Goya Foods born of a job lost

Just inside Goya Foods' headquarters [in Secaucus, New Jersey], a sepia-toned mural tells the history of the company's founders. It shows how patriarch [head of the family] Prudencio Unanue immigrated from his native Spain to Puerto Rico in 1904 and to New York in 1915. There, he established what has become the largest Hispanic-owned food company in the USA.

For two decades, Prudencio worked odd jobs in the food industry before he got on with a Spanish importer of olives and canned sardines. Then the Spanish Civil War started, halting trade and throwing Prudencio out of a job.

Unemployed, desperation became his inspiration, recalls his son, Joseph. "He had to do something. We had four kids and we had to eat."

Homesick for the foods of Spain and Puerto Rico, Unanue believed Puerto Ricans, Cubans and other Caribbean immigrants were too. So in 1936, he and his wife, Carolina, also of Spanish descent, started Goya Foods, the name borrowed from the sardine label he had imported.

In 1992 [Goya Foods' annual] revenue was $453 million, making it the USA's largest Hispanic-owned business. The Unanues are also among the wealthiest Hispanic families in the U.S. with a net worth estimated at $330 million. But wealth hasn't come easily to the Unanue clan. Most have worked to make Goya a giant brand name.

Joseph, 68, who took over in

When Mexicans moved to the United States, most left their traditional cooking tools behind. In their new, often cramped, homes, they didn't have space to cook traditional Mexican meals. They didn't have large open-air ovens. Often they did not have the money to buy meat. So they cooked with cheaper foods such as beans and rice. In

1977, is president. Brother Frank, 61, is president of Goya de Puerto Rico. Their children and the children of their brother Charles and their deceased brother, Anthony, virtually all work for the company.

Prudencio died in 1977; Carolina in 1984. Were they still around, they probably wouldn't believe what their offspring are up to. The second- and third-generation Unanues are shaking up Goya's mainstay Caribbean product mix with M&M: mainstream and Mexican. And they aren't overlooking the waves of immigrants from the Dominican Republic, Central and Latin America.

Coping with these different tastes means a serious expansion of Goya's product line, because Hispanics of Mexican and Central American descent enjoy foods unfamiliar to Hispanics of Caribbean descent—and vice versa. In fact, Goya introduced its first salsa in 1990—Goya Salsa Picante Sauce—which it hopes will one day be as big as Heinz ketchup.

That may not be as difficult as it sounds, because the market for ethnic foods is hot. While overall supermarket revenue has been flat for several years, revenue of Mexican foods sold at supermarkets has doubled to $2.2 billion since 1987.

But Goya faces stiff competition: Major U.S. food companies, which market to mainstream America, dominate the Mexican foods market. In the sauces category, Pace Foods is No. 1. Pet's Old Al Paso is No. 2. And with rapid growth in the U.S. Hispanic population more major food companies are getting into the act.

"Obviously, they're doing something right to be where they are," says Maria Ibias, [the advertising director at Iberia, a food distributor for the Hispanic American market]. "But we're following in their footsteps." To stay ahead of competitors, Goya must protect its market share in Hispanic-owned stores while increasing its presence in the mainstream. Both will be difficult in the '90s, says Smith Barney food industry analyst Ron Morrow. "Goya has been a strong regional label. It is not strong as you go nationwide. But Goya can do well if it doesn't try to cover too much territory."

—*Rhonda Richards*

barrios across the United States, Mexican grocery stores sold mostly tortillas, cornmeal, beans, and rice.

New styles of cooking sprang up in areas close to the Mexican–U.S. border. In Texas, Tex-Mex food is common. Chili with meat, or chili con carne, is a Tex-Mex staple. But it's not really Mexican.

Mexican Americans living in Texas around 1880 first made it. In 1908 a German American got the idea of selling chili con carne in cans. The new food took off across the U.S. Southwest.

These days, Mexican Americans live in every part of the United States. And it's easy to find every version of Mexican food in most states as well.

COLORFUL CUBAN AMERICAN COOKING

Cuban food is a flavorful, colorful combination of Spanish and African cooking styles. Black beans, rice, and garlic are common ingredients. Cubans also add local tropical fruits such as bananas and pineapples to many dishes. Fried sliced bananas are a popular dessert. Many Cuban dishes also contain root vegetables such as yucca. Yucca is similar to potatoes.

Cuban restaurants are found throughout the United States. They are most popular in areas where a lot of Cubans have settled. South Florida has the largest population of Cuban Americans. Hundreds of Cuban restaurants are found in Miami and nearby cities.

Baked Eggs

Many Cubans like to eat baked eggs for breakfast. Try making these baked eggs in your own kitchen.

INGREDIENTS
¼ cup olive oil
3 cloves garlic, peeled and minced
1 large onion, chopped
1 large green bell pepper, seeded and chopped
1 large tomato, chopped, or 1 8-ounce can diced tomatoes
salt and pepper to taste
6 eggs
3 tablespoons butter, melted

PREPARATION
1. Preheat oven to 350ºF.
2. In a large, deep skillet, heat oil over medium heat. Sauté garlic, onion, and green pepper for 2 to 3 minutes, or until onion is soft but not brown. Add tomato and cook 15 minutes, or until sauce thickens. Add salt and pepper to taste.
3. Lightly oil six ramekins (small ceramic serving dishes). Divide sauce evenly among ramekins. Break 1 egg into each dish, being careful not to break the yolk. Drizzle a bit of melted butter over each egg.
4. Place dishes in oven. Bake for 10 to 12 minutes, or until the whites of the eggs are completely white and the yolks are still a bit runny.
5. Remove from oven. Season with more salt and pepper if desired. Serve immediately.

Serves 6

They're usually owned and operated by first-, second-, or third-generation Cuban Americans. Many of their customers are Cuban immigrants, but they are also immensely popular with tourists who want a little taste of Cuba.

PUERTO RICAN FAVORITES

Puerto Rican food has a lot in common with Cuban and other Caribbean cooking styles. Puerto Rican cooking is influenced by both Spanish and African traditions. Like Cubans, Puerto Ricans base many of their meals on black beans, rice, tropical fruit, and vegetables such as yucca. Chicken and pork are favorite meats. But Puerto Ricans have their own special dishes. One is *mofongo*, which includes beans, rice, and plantains (a type of banana). Another is *asopao*, a chicken and rice dish.

Puerto Ricans in large cities can often find the ingredients needed for favorite dishes at their local grocery stores. At home, their families can enjoy traditional Puerto Rican meals. Puerto Ricans in smaller towns or rural areas may have to improvise to get a taste of home. For example, they may have to substitute traditional ingredients for ones that are more readily available.

From Mexican mole to Puerto Rican mofongo, variety defines Hispanic American dining. The rich palette of colors and flavors is as diverse as Hispanic Americans themselves. By cooking and enjoying this diverse array of foods, Hispanic Americans can connect with their traditional cultures.

A traditional meal of Puerto Rican food may consist of black beans, rice, and plantains.

Coconut Flan

Flan is a rich custard dessert. Coconut flan is a special favorite of many Hispanic diners. Try this tasty coconut flan recipe. You might want to ask an adult to help you.

INGREDIENTS

1 cup granulated sugar

6 eggs

1 12-ounce can evaporated milk

1 14-ounce can coconut milk

1 14-ounce can sweetened condensed milk

1 tablespoon vanilla extract

PREPARATION

1. Preheat oven to 350°F.
2. Caramelize sugar in a 9 x 9-inch baking pan by pouring sugar into the pan and placing over low heat. Move the pan continuously to prevent burning. When sugar begins to bubble, remove pan from heat and turn it so the glaze covers the bottom of the pan. Cool.
3. In a large bowl, beat eggs lightly, and add remaining ingredients. Beat until well blended.
4. Pour egg mixture through a strainer into the prepared (and cooled) pan.
5. Place pan in a larger pan that is filled with enough hot water to come about halfway up the side of the prepared pan. Place in oven, and bake 45 to 50 minutes, or until toothpick inserted in center comes out clean.
6. Remove from oven, and separate the pans. Allow flan to cool on a rack.
7. To serve, dip the bottom of the pan in warm water and invert onto a serving platter.

Makes 8 to 10 servings

FAMOUS HISPANIC AMERICANS

Christina Aguilera

(b. 1980) Pop star Christina Aguilera was born in Staten Island, New York. Her father is from Ecuador. When she was twelve, she joined the cast of the television show the *Mickey Mouse Club*. She became well known for her singing and dancing. At eighteen she signed her first recording contract with RCA Records.

Aguilera's career took off after her first album was released. Over the next ten years, she released six more albums, including a Spanish-language album in 2000.

Aguilera married music executive Jason Bratman in November 2005. On January 12, 2008, she gave birth to a son, Max Liron Bratman.

Desi Arnaz

(1917–1986) This star of the 1950s television hit *I Love Lucy* was born in Cuba. His father was a member of the Cuban government in the early 1930s. When Cuban citizens overthrew the government in 1933, Arnaz's father was sent to prison. The entire family eventually fled to the United States.

Arnaz got his break acting on Broadway in 1939. He spent the next ten years in Hollywood. He appeared in several movies and met his wife, Lucille Ball, on the set of the movie *Too Many Girls*. In 1951 Arnaz and Ball launched the *I Love Lucy* show, which went on to become one of television's most popular sitcoms ever. The couple later formed a production company and enjoyed much success. They had two children together and divorced in 1960. Arnaz remarried and remained in show business until he died of lung cancer in 1986.

Cesar Chavez

(1927–1993) Mexican American labor activist Cesar Chavez was born near Yuma, Arizona. He quit school after eighth grade to help support his family. Chavez earned money picking grapes as a migrant farmworker. Migrant farmworkers moved from town to town and worked long hours. They had few rights and received little pay.

Chavez was disgusted with the working conditions that migrant farmworkers faced. As an adult, he formed a union (a group that supports workers' rights) to help the migrant workers. He also organized strikes—work stoppages meant to force employers to meet a union's demands. Chavez improved conditions for migrant farmworkers. In 1994, one year after his death, President Bill Clinton honored Chavez with a Presidential Medal of Freedom—a prize that goes to citizens whose life's work betters the United States.

Oscar Hijuelos

(b. 1951) Award-winning author Oscar Hijuelos was born to Cuban immigrants in New York City. He became the first Hispanic to win the Pulitzer Prize for Fiction. Hijuelos earned bachelor's and master's degrees in writing from the City College of New York. He worked at an advertising firm from 1977 to 1984 but spent his evenings writing fiction.

Hijuelos's first novel, *Our House in the Last World*, was published in 1983. His second novel, *The Mambo Kings Play Songs of Love*, won the 1990 Pulitzer Prize. It tells the story of Cuban brothers who immigrate to the United States in the early 1950s. The book was made into a movie in 1992. In 2005 it became a Broadway musical.

Ellen Ochoa

(b. 1958) Ellen Ochoa was the first Hispanic American female astronaut. Ochoa was born in Los Angeles, California, to Mexican American parents. Her parents divorced when she was in high school, and she lived with her mother, brothers, and sister in La Mesa, California.

Ochoa received her doctorate degree in engineering from Stanford University in 1985. She became the first Hispanic woman in space in 1993, when she went up on a nine-day mission aboard the shuttle *Discovery*. Ochoa later became the director of flight crew operations for the National Aeronautics and Space Administration (NASA).

Sonia Sotomayor

(b. 1954) U.S. Supreme Court justice Sonia Sotomayor is the nation's first Hispanic Supreme Court justice. Sotomayor was born in New York City to Puerto Rican immigrants. After her father died when she was nine, her mother worked two jobs to support her family. Sotomayor graduated from Princeton University in 1976 and received her law degree from Yale in 1979.

In 1992 Sotomayor became a U.S. district court judge for the Southern District of New York. In 1998 she became a circuit judge for the U.S. Court of Appeals for the Second Circuit. She served in that role for more than ten years before she was nominated by President Barack Obama to replace retiring U.S. Supreme Court justice David Souter. On August 6, 2009, she was confirmed for this new job by the U.S. Senate. She took the oath of office three days later.

EXPLORE YOUR HERITAGE

Where did your family come from? Who are your relatives, and where do they live? Were they born in the United States? If not, when and why did they come here? Where did you get your family name? Is it German? Puerto Rican? Vietnamese? Something else? If you are adopted, what is your adoptive family's story?

By searching for the answers to these questions, you can begin to discover your family's history. And if your family history is hard to trace, team up with a friend to share ideas or to learn more about that person's family history.

Where to Start

Start with what you know. In a notebook or on your family's computer, write down the full names of the relatives you know about and anything you know about them—where they lived, what they liked to do as children, any awards or honors they earned, and so on.

Next, gather some primary sources. Primary sources are the records and observations of eyewitnesses to events. They include diaries; letters; autobiographies; speeches; newspapers; birth, marriage, and death records; photographs; and ship records. The best primary resources about your family may be in family scrapbooks or files in your home or in your relatives' homes. You may also find some interesting material in libraries, archives, historical societies, and museums. These organizations often have primary sources available online.

The Next Steps

After taking notes and gathering primary sources, think about what facts and details you are missing. You can then prepare to interview your relatives to see if they can fill in these gaps. First, write down any questions that you would like to ask them about their lives. Then ask your relatives if they would mind being interviewed. Don't be upset if they say no. Understand that some people do not like to talk about their pasts.

Also, consider interviewing family friends. They can often provide interesting stories and details about your relatives. They might have photographs too.

Family Interviews

When you are ready for an interview, gather your questions, a notepad, a tape recorder or camcorder, and any other materials you might need. Consider showing your interview subjects a photograph or a timetable of important events at the start of your interview. These items can help jog the memory of your subjects and get them talking. You might also bring U.S. and world maps to an interview. Ask your subjects to label the places they have lived.

Remember that people's memories aren't always accurate. Sometimes they forget information and confuse dates. You might want to take a trip to the library or look online to check dates and other facts.

Get Organized!

When you finish your interviews and research, you are ready to organize your information. There are many ways of doing this. You can write a history of your entire family or individual biographies of your relatives. You can create a timeline going back to your earliest known ancestors. You can make a family tree—a diagram or chart that shows how people in your family are related to one another.

If you have collected a lot of photographs, consider compiling a photo album or scrapbook that tells your family history. Or if you used a camcorder to record your interviews, you might even want to make a movie.

However you put together your family history, be sure to share it! Your relatives will want to see all the information you found. You might want to create a website or blog so that other people can learn about your family. Whatever you choose to do, you'll end up with something your family will appreciate for years to come.

HISPANIC AMERICAN SNAPSHOT

This chart shows a statistical snapshot of people from five main countries or territories from which Hispanic Americans have immigrated. It looks at how many Hispanic Americans from each place are living in the United States and which places have the greatest population.

For more information on Hispanic American populations, see the 2000 U.S. Census data at http://factfinder.census.gov.

HISPANIC AMERICAN GROUP	TOTAL U.S. POPULATION	FIVE TOP STATES OF RESIDENCE
Mexicans	28,339,354	California: 8,600,581 Texas: 5,179,899 Illinois: 1,154,554 Arizona: 1,083,524 Florida: 358,123
Puerto Ricans	3,403,510	New York: 1,047,866 Florida: 481,337 New Jersey: 369,231 Pennsylvania: 230,914 Massachusetts: 200,001
Cubans	1,520,276	Florida: 846,080 New Jersey: 78,995 California: 70,623 New York: 62,753 Texas: 27,034
El Salvadorans	1,371,666	California: 296,113 Texas: 88,605 New York: 76,185 Virginia: 48,482 Maryland: 37,094
Dominicans	1,217,225	New York: 474,300 New Jersey: 104,800 Florida: 73,539 Massachusetts: 53,350 Rhode Island: 18,874

GLOSSARY

Advent: the Christmas season as marked by the coming (birth) of Jesus. Advent begins four Sundays before Christmas Day. Many Hispanic Americans observe Advent by going to church, enjoying family festivities, and giving gifts.

assimilation: blending into a society's mainstream culture

barrio: a Spanish-speaking community or neighborhood

Chicano: a word to describe someone or something of Mexican descent in the United States

Cinco de Mayo: the fifth of May; a holiday celebrating the day that Mexicans fought back French invaders in 1862

descendant: a person born of a certain ancestor, family, or group. Most Hispanic Americans are descendants of Spanish settlers and Native Americans.

futbol: the name for soccer in Spanish-speaking countries. Futbol is the national sport in most of Latin America.

Good Friday: the day on which Christians believe Jesus died. Good Friday comes two days before Easter.

Holy Week: the week before Easter

Latin America: the name for a huge region that includes all the land in the Western Hemisphere south of the United States

mole: a spicy sauce made with chilies and usually chocolate that is served with meat

plantain: a type of banana

quinceañera: a girl's fifteenth birthday celebration. The age of fifteen is considered the beginning of adulthood for girls in Latin America.

reggaeton: a style of Puerto Rican hip-hop music

rock en Español: rock music with Spanish lyrics

Roman Catholicism: a Christian religion whose followers believe in one God and attend worship services called Mass. Most Hispanic Americans are Roman Catholic.

Tejano music: music that combines elements of traditional Mexican music, rock music, and country music

Three Kings Day: a Latin American holiday celebrating the day that Christians believe three kings arrived with gifts for the baby Jesus. Three Kings Day is on January 6.

tortilla: a thin round of cornmeal or wheat flour bread

xenophobic: fearful of or prejudiced against foreign people and languages

yucca: a starchy root vegetable, similar to a potato

SELECTED BIBLIOGRAPHY

Garver, Susan, and Paula McGuire. *Coming to North America from Mexico, Cuba and Puerto Rico.* New York: Delacorte Press, 1981.
This book describes the immigration of three groups of Hispanic Americans.

Gonzales, Manuel G. *Mexicanos: A History of Mexicans in the United States.* Bloomington: Indiana University Press, 1999.
This title examines the long history of Mexicans in the United States.

McNerney, Eileen. *A Story of Suffering and Hope: Lessons from Latino Youth.* Mahwah, NJ: Paulist Press, 2005.
McNerney examines the troubles many young Hispanic Americans face.

Meier, Matt S., and Feliciano Ribera. *Mexican Americans, American Mexicans: From Conquistadors to Chicanos.* New York: Hill and Wang, 1993.
Meier and Ribera provide background information on Mexican Americans.

Menard, Valerie. *The Latino Holiday Book: From Cinco de Mayo to Dia de los Muertos: The Celebrations and Traditions of Hispanic-Americans.* New York: Treasure Chest Books, 2000.
This book offers useful information on Hispanic American holidays and celebrations.

Sandoval, Moises. *On the Move: A History of the Hispanic Church in the United States.* Maryknoll, NY: Orbis Books, 2006.
This book gives extensive details on Hispanic American religious worship.

U.S. Census Bureau. *Language Use and English-Speaking Ability: 2000. Census 2000 Brief.* August 26, 2008. http://www.census.gov/population/www/cen2000/phc-t20.html (July 8, 2009).
The U.S. Census Bureau provides information on the language use of immigrants to the United States.

FURTHER READING AND WEBSITES

Alegre, Cesar. *Extraordinary Hispanic Americans.* New York: Children's Press, 2007.
Read about a wide array of famous Hispanic Americans, from labor activist Cesar Chavez to popular singing star Selena.

Behnke, Alison. *Cooking the Central American Way.* Minneapolis: Lerner Publications Company, 2005.
This cookbook has photos and recipes from different areas of Central America as well as information on the culture and land in the region.

——. *Cooking the Cuban Way.* Minneapolis: Lerner Publications Company, 2004.
This illustrated cookbook features many Cuban recipes plus interesting facts about Cuba.

——. *Mexicans in America.* Minneapolis: Lerner Publications Company, 2005.
Learn more about the history and culture of Mexican Americans.

Campbell, Kumari. *Cuba in Pictures.* Minneapolis: Twenty-First Century Books, 2005.
Explore Cuba—a nation to which many Hispanic Americans can trace their heritage.

Cisneros, Sandra. *The House on Mango Street.* New York: Vintage Books, 1991.
This novel for young adults tells the story of a Mexican American girl's life in the United States.

Collins, David R. *Cesar Chavez*. Minneapolis: Lerner Publications Company, 2005.
Read this biography of Hispanic American Cesar Chavez and learn more about his work on behalf of laborers.

Coronado, Rose. *Cooking the Mexican Way*. Minneapolis: Lerner Publications Company, 2002.
This illustrated cookbook presents recipes from Mexico as well as information on the country.

Enchanted Learning: Cesar Chavez Biography
http://www.enchantedlearning.com/history/us/hispanicamerican/chavez
This website offers a biography of Cesar Chavez and a selection of activities related to the labor leader.

Hamilton, Janice. *Mexico in Pictures*. Minneapolis: Twenty-First Century Books, 2003.
Read all about Mexico—the country from which the majority of Hispanic Americans came.

Márquez, Herón. *Latin Sensations*. Minneapolis: Twenty-First Century Books, 2001.
Learn all about successful Hispanic American entertainers such as Jennifer Lopez, Ricky Martin, and Selena in this book from the A&E Biography series.

McElroy, Lisa Tucker. *Sonia Sotomayor: First Hispanic U.S. Supreme Court Justice*. Minneapolis: Lerner Publications Company, 2010.
This biography of Sonia Sotomayor traces her life from her upbringing in the Bronx, New York, to her appointment to the U.S. Supreme Court.

Mexican Folklore
http://www.americanfolklore.net/mexican-folklore.html
This site features engaging stories that are popular throughout Mexico and Hispanic American communities.

Rice, David. *Crazy Loco*. New York: Dial Books, 2001.
This collection of short stories describes the lives of several young Hispanic Americans.

Smithsonian Latino Center's Kids Corner
http://latino.si.edu/KidsCorner/index.html
Explore Latino cultural traditions in music, art, and more at this interactive website for kids.

Taus-Bolstad, Stacy. *Puerto Ricans in America*. Minneapolis: Lerner Publications Company, 2005.
This book investigates the history of Puerto Ricans on the mainland United States. It also offers a look at present-day Puerto Rican American culture.

Thornley, Stew. *Roberto Clemente*. Minneapolis: Twenty-First Century Books, 2007.
Read about the Hispanic American baseball great in this book in the Sports Heroes and Legends series.

INDEX

USA TODAY
CULTURAL MOSAIC

PHOTO ACKNOWLEDGMENTS

The images in this book are used with the permission of: © David McNew/Getty Images, pp. 3 (top), 4; © MPI/Hulton Archive/Getty Images, pp. 3 (second from top), 6; © Victor Calzada/USA TODAY, pp. 3 (third from top), 20; AP Photo/Mark J. Terrill, pp. 3 (middle), 34; © CJ Gunther/USA TODAY, pp. 3 (third from bottom), 43; © Joel Salcido/USA TODAY, pp. 3 (second from bottom), 50; © David Bishop Inc./FoodPix/Getty Images, pp. 3 (bottom), 68; © Topham/The Image Works, p. 7; AP Photo/Reed Saxon, p. 11; © Adam Gerik/USA TODAY, p. 12; © Jack Gruber/USA TODAY, pp. 14, 27; © Underwood Photo Archives/SuperStock, p. 15 (left); AP Photo/Fresno Bee, Mark Crosse, p. 15 (right); © Steve Snowden/Getty Images, p. 16; AP Photo/Eric Gay, p. 17; AP Photo/Julie Jacobson, p. 18; © Christopher Peterson/BuzzFoto/FilmMagic/Getty Images, p. 19; © Dan MacMedan/USA TODAY, pp. 22, 26, 59; AP Photo/Paul Howell, Houston Chronicle, p. 23; © Bob Riha, Jr./ USA TODAY, pp. 25 (top), 70 (top); AP Photo, pp. 25 (bottom), 35; AP Photo/Chris Pizzello, p. 28; © Andy Holzman/Los Angeles Daily News/ZUMA Press, p. 29; AP Photo/Kirkland, p. 30; © Emmanuel Aguirre/Getty Images, p. 31 (left); © Janette Pellegrini/Getty Images, p. 31 (right); © Robert Hanashiro/USA TODAY, p. 32; © Robert Deutsch/USA TODAY, p. 36; © Alex Wong/Getty Images, p. 37 (top); © Doug Pensinger/Getty Images, p. 38; © Eileen Blass/USA TODAY, p. 40; AP Photo/David J. Phillip, p. 41; AP Photo/Charlie Riedel, p. 42; © Richard Cummins/SuperStock, p. 44; © Mark Rightmire/The Orange County Register/ ZUMA Press, p. 46; AP Photo/Ross D. Franklin, p. 47; © Jack Hollingsworth/Digital Vision/ Getty Images, p. 52 (top); © Thomas Northcut/Photodisc/Getty Images, p. 52 (bottom); AP Photo/Bob Child, p. 53; © Sandy Huffaker/Getty Images, p. 56; © Axiom Photographic Limited/SuperStock, p. 57; © Scott Boehm/Getty Images, p. 58; © Robert Harding Picture Library/SuperStock, p. 60; © Omar Torres/AFP/Getty Images, p. 62; © Whiteplaid/ Dreamstime.com, p. 63 (top); AP Photo/Janet Hostetter, p. 66; © Martin Jacobs/StockFood Creative/Getty Images, p. 69; © Hulton Archive/Getty Images, p. 70 (middle); AP Photo/ Alan Greth, p. 70 (bottom); AP Photo/NASA, Bill Ingalls, p. 71 (middle); © Ulf Andersen/ Getty Images, p. 71 (top); © H. Darr Beiser/USA TODAY, p. 71 (bottom); © Todd Strand/ Independent Picture Service, pp. 72-73.
Front Cover: © John & Lisa Merrill/Stone/Getty Images (left); © Bob Daemmrich/The Image Works (top right); © iStockphoto.com/Gema Blanton (bottom right).

ABOUT THE AUTHOR

Children's and YA author Sandy Donovan has written numerous titles for Lerner Publishing Group, including *Running for Office: A Look at Political Campaigns, Iranians in America*, and three titles in USA TODAY's Cultural Mosaic series. Donovan is a graduate of the Humphrey Institute of Public Policy at the University of Minnesota and lives in Minneapolis, Minnesota.